Ants

By Christy Steele

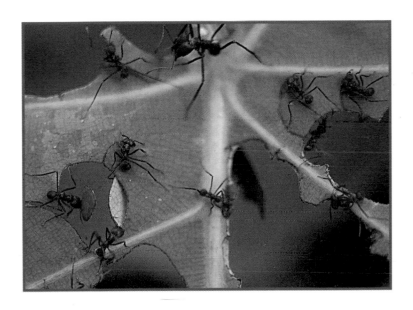

STECK-VAUGHN
ELEMENTARY · SECONDARY · ADULT · LIBRARY

A Harcourt Company

www.steck-vaughn.com

ANIMALS OF THE RAIN FOREST

Photo Acknowledgments
Kevin Schafer, cover
USDA-ARS, 4–5, 11, 20, 25 (left and right)
Visuals Unlimited/D. Cavagnaro, title page; Milton Tierney, 8;
    Nancy Wells, 12; Brian Rogers, 14; Walt Anderson, 16;
    Glenn M. Oliver, 18; David Ellis, 22; Don Fawcett, 26;
    George Loun, 29.

Contents

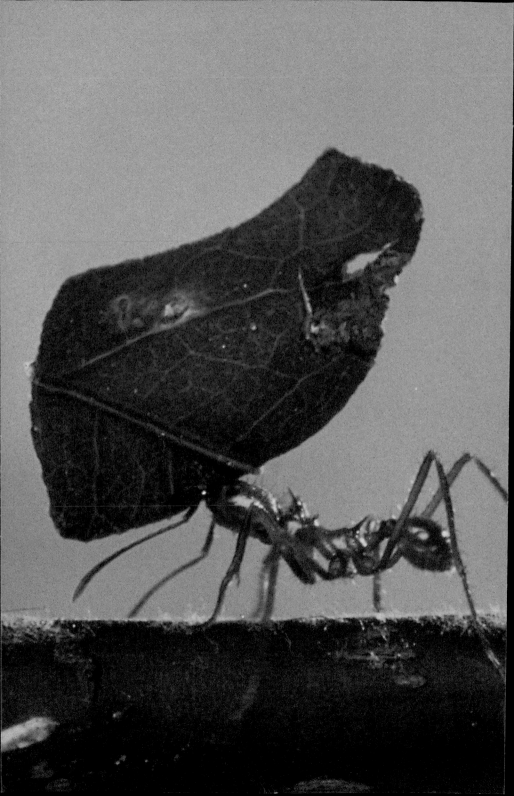

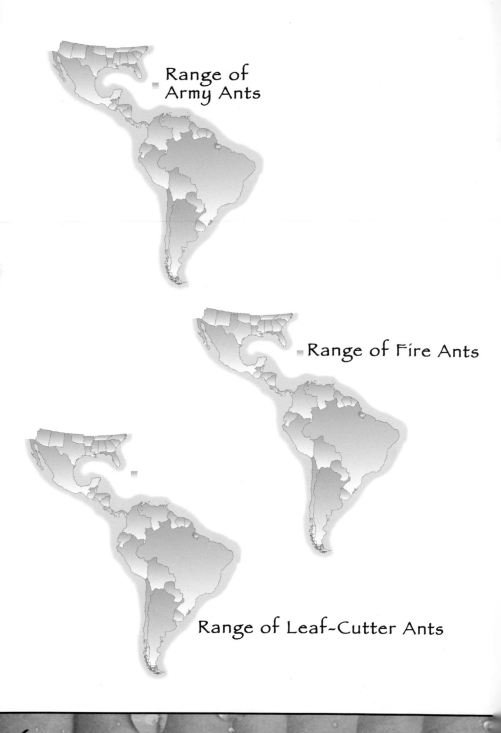

Range of
Army Ants

Range of Fire Ants

Range of Leaf-Cutter Ants

A Quick Look at Ants

What do ants look like?
Ants are insects. They
have three main body
sections, six legs, and
two antennas.

Where do ants live?
The ants featured in this book live on the ground or
in underground nests in and around rain forests.

What do ants eat?
Leaf-cutter ants eat a special kind of fungus. Army
ants eat meat. Fire ants eat meat, seeds, and nectar.
Nectar is a sweet liquid found in flowers.

Do ants have any enemies?
Armadillos, anteaters, spiders, birds, and many other
animals and insects eat ants.

These leaf-cutter ants are bringing new leaf pieces to their nest.

Ants in the Rain Forest

There are thousands of known kinds of ants in the world. Most of these ants live in warm rain forests. Scientists believe that rain forests are home to even more kinds of ants that scientists have not found yet.

Ants are an important part of the life cycle of the rain forest. They eat rain forest plants, other insects, and nectar. Nectar is a sweet liquid found in flowers. But ants are also food for other animals. Armadillos, anteaters, and many other animals eat ants.

This book is about army ants, fire ants, and leaf-cutter ants. These kinds of ants live in many places in South and Central America. Many ants live in Amazonia. This is the largest rain forest in the world. It grows around the Amazon River.

Appearance

All ants have things in common. Ants have six legs. They all have bodies with three main sections. The first section of an ant's body is the head. The heads of each kind of ant are different sizes and shapes.

All ant heads have body parts that help ants sense the world around them. Antennas are feelers that grow on the top of an ant's head. Ants use antennas to touch, smell, and taste. Most ants have eyes, but many are blind or cannot see well.

Ants have powerful outer jaws called mandibles. Mandibles move differently than people's jaws. They move side to side like scissors instead of up and down. Ants use mandibles to fight, to dig nests, to bite, and to carry things, such as their food or their young.

The thorax is the middle part of an ant's body. An ant's six legs attach to the thorax.

Fire ants have a thorax that is thinner than the head.

The back section of an ant's body is its abdomen. It contains two stomachs. Ants use one stomach to break down food they swallow. They use the other stomach to store some of their food. They bring food from this second stomach back up into their mouths to feed other ants. Some kinds of ants have stingers on the end of the abdomen.

Some worker ants are in charge of digging and fixing the colony's nest.

Life in the Colony

Ants are social insects. This means they live and work together in groups called colonies. Each ant has a special job to do.

The queen is a female ant that heads the colony. The queen's only job is to mate and lay eggs. All the other ants in the colony take care of the queen.

Drones are the only male ants in a colony. Their one job is to mate with a queen. Drones die when they are finished mating.

 Ants give off special scents, or odors, to send messages to other ants. They pass the scents by licking other ants or releasing the scents into the air. Some scents tell other ants when they are in danger. Other scents lead ants to food. Scents help members of a colony know each other. Soldier ants smell each ant trying to enter the colony. The soldier will fight an ant that does not carry the colony's special scent.

Some kinds of ants have soldier ants that guard and protect the colony. Soldiers are bigger than the other ants. They often have larger mandibles to fight enemies. Enemy ants sometimes try to steal the colony's food. Other kinds of ants may take ants they catch back to their own colony to work.

Worker ants do many jobs in the colony. They feed the queen. They take care of eggs and larvas. Larvas are newly hatched ants. Nurse ants lick the eggs and larvas to keep them clean. Worker ants clean the nest by carrying waste outside it. Some workers build a nest for the ant colony. Other workers look for food. These workers are called scouts or foragers.

▲ **Ants can carry objects that are up to 50 times their body weight. This worker ant will live for several months.**

Life Cycle

Ants all have the same life cycle. They go through three times of growth called stages.

It usually takes ants about 30 days to grow from egg to larva to pupa to adult. The eggs, larvas, and pupas of a colony are called its brood.

An ant spends the first part of its life in an egg. After time, the egg hatches. Each kind of ant egg hatches at a different time.

A young larva comes out of the egg. Larvas are small and wormlike. Worker ants feed and clean the larvas. Larvas eat and grow. They can stay in this stage from a few weeks to several months.

To enter the pupa stage, larvas spin cocoons around themselves. Inside these silky coverings, the larva turns into a pupa that looks like a fully formed adult ant. When the pupa is fully developed, it breaks out of its cocoon. It is then an adult ant.

All ants work in the colony. Young adult ants begin life by becoming nurses. They take care of the growing brood. After time, they begin other kinds of work. The oldest ants in the colony are the scout ants that look for food.

Most worker ants live for several months. Drones live for about one month. Queens live up to eight years or more.

People leave their villages when a column of army ants arrives. They come back after the ants have eaten all the insects and traveled to a new place.

Army Ants

There are about 150 kinds of army ants. They are strong, meat-eating ants. They eat mostly insects. But they will also eat any other animal they can kill. They have strong jaws and can grow up to 1 inch (2.5 cm) long.

Army ants form long, wide lines as they move. A column of army ants can be up to one-half mile (.8 km) long. The way these ants travel looks like soldiers marching in an army. So people named them army ants.

Army ants live in huge colonies of up to 1 million ants. A large colony of army ants can eat up to 100,000 insects a day. They eat all the insects in one area quickly. The colony is always moving to look for more food.

▲ **Army ants may travel up to 217 feet (350 m) from their nest to look for food.**

Army Ant Nests

Army ants do not build permanent nests because they are always moving. Each night, they build a temporary nest called a bivouac. The bivouac is a long, living chain of ants. Each ant hooks its mandibles and the claws on its legs to another ant in the colony. The chain of ants wraps itself around the queen and the younger ants. In the morning, the ants unhook themselves and start moving again.

Army ants stay in one place for several days when larvas are spinning their cocoons to turn into pupas. At this time, the queen lays new eggs in the center of the bivouac. The colony begins moving again only when the eggs hatch into larvas.

Hunting

Army ants use scents to find food. All the workers are blind. A scout leads a column of ants to look for food. They move forward by following the scout's scent trails.

Army ants hunt in two ways. Sometimes the ants walk forward in a thick column. Small groups of ants move out in different directions from the main column. From overhead, this looks like a tree. Other times, a huge group of ants makes a fanlike shape and sweeps forward through the rain forest.

Once they have found food, many army ants crawl over the animal or insect. Their strong jaws bite small pieces off the animal. A group of army ants can turn an animal into a pile of bones in just a few hours.

People named these ants fire ants because their stings burn like fire.

Fire Ants

There are many different kinds of fire ants. Each kind lives in its own special habitat. A habitat is where an animal usually lives and grows. Fire ants can live in grasslands, flood plains, or lightly forested places in Amazonia.

Fire ants are small. They grow up to one-quarter inch (.6 cm) long. Their color ranges from red-brown to black. Some people fear fire ants because of their painful stings.

Unlike army ants, fire ants build underground nests that last a long time. Their nests are about 1 to 2 feet (.3 to .6 m) wide and several feet deep. The ants dig a series of large, roomlike areas called chambers. They dig tunnels to connect the chambers. A pile of loose soil is left over the nest after the ants are done digging.

Fire ants are scavengers, too. They will eat animals that they did not kill, such as this bird.

Hunting and Eating

Fire ants eat other insects as well as plants and animals. They eat other ants. They also eat grains and seeds. Large groups of fire ants can eat most of the seeds that a farmer has planted to grow a crop.

A fire ant scout hunts for any kind of food it can find. Sometimes it finds food that is too large for it to carry back to the nest. Then it leaves a scent trail to lead other workers to the prey. Prey are the animals and insects that fire ants eat.

Fire ants catch prey by stinging. First, they grab onto their prey with their mandibles. Then the fire ants use the stingers on their abdomens to sting the prey. Each sting puts venom into the prey's body. The venom is a poison that slows down insects and animals. This makes the animals unable to run away from the ants.

The sting of one fire ant would not be enough to hurt most animals. So they sting the animals together. The combined venom of thousands of fire ants can slow down even large animals, such as young deer. Even so, most healthy animals can still escape from fire ants. Young or sick animals are in the most danger.

Fire ants then eat the animals they catch. They drink the juice and blood from their prey. In just one day, a group of fire ants can eat all of an animal but its bones.

Colony Wars

Each fire-ant colony has its own nest. They rush out of the nest and sting anything that comes too close to it.

Each colony also has its own territory. A territory is a space the ants know well. The ants live and hunt in the colony's territory. Fire ants will fight to protect their territory.

A fire-ant colony will sometimes fight another one for more territory. This happens when many fire-ant colonies live close together in a small space. There may not be enough food for all the fire-ant colonies. Then workers might enter another colony's territory to look for food. This starts a fight between the colonies.

Fire-ant colonies are small when they are first formed. Sometimes many new, small fire-ant colonies are close together. One of the new colonies may try to grow larger by stealing broods from other colonies. This causes a fight. Workers in the winning colony will enter the losing colony's nest and carry out the brood. When the ants hatch, they become workers for the winning colony.

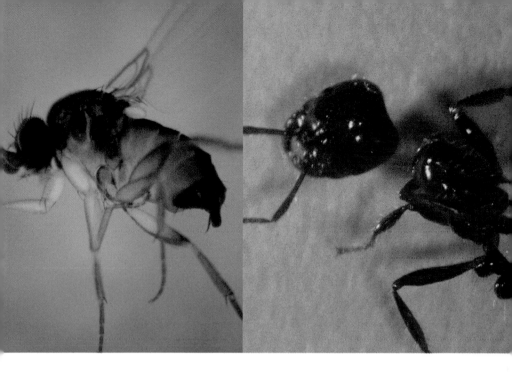

A phorid fly (left) lays eggs in fire ants' heads. This fire ant died after a phorid-fly larva became a pupa (right).

Phorid Flies

One of the biggest enemies of the fire ant is the phorid fly. A phorid fly lays an egg in a fire ant's head. After time, the egg hatches. The larva lives in the ant's head. When the fly larva enters its pupa stage, the fire ant's head falls off. The ant dies.

Leaf-cutter ants are nicknamed umbrella ants because the leaf pieces they carry look like umbrellas.

Leaf-Cutter Ants

Unlike army ants and fire ants, leaf-cutter ants do not eat meat or insects. Instead, they eat a special kind of fungus that grows only in their nests. A fungus is a plantlike living thing that feeds on rotting matter.

Leaf-cutter ants dig huge underground nests with many large chambers. Chambers can be up to 3 feet (.9 m) wide. They dig tunnels to connect the chambers together. They also dig special tunnels to let in outside air.

Leaf-cutter ants use the chambers to grow the fungus that they eat. The ants are like farmers. They make sure there is enough heat and water for the fungus to grow.

Fungus Gardens

A queen leaf-cutter ant starts a colony's fungus garden. She carries a piece of fungus with her when she leaves her old colony. She picks a new place and digs a small tunnel and chamber for herself. She places the piece of fungus in the chamber and puts special juices on the fungus to make it grow.

The queen then lays eggs. Once the eggs have turned into adult ants, some of the new workers dig more rooms and tunnels in the nest. Other workers leave the nest to find leaves. They use their mandibles to cut circles from the leaves. Then they carry these leaf pieces back to the nest.

The ants prepare the leaves. They lick the leaves to clean them. At night, the ants place leaves that are too dry outside to get wet. During the day, the ants put leaves that are too wet in the sun to dry.

Leaf-cutter ants begin chewing the leaves when they are just right for growing fungus. They spit out the chewed leaves and put them in the chambers. The fungus grows on the chewed, rotting leaves.

▲ These leaf pieces will become food for the fungus.

Destroying the Rain Forest

The rain forest is home to thousands of other kinds of ants besides leaf-cutter ants, fire ants, and army ants. In some places, people are tearing down the rain forest to log, to farm, to raise cattle, or to build homes. Ant colonies will only live as long as people do not destroy the rain forest.

Glossary

abdomen (AB-duh-muhn)—the back section of an insect's body

Amazonia (am-uh-ZONE-ee-uh)—the largest rain forest in the world

antenna (an-TEN-uh)—a body part on the head of some insects that allows them to touch, taste, and smell objects around them

brood (BROOD)—a group of young; the eggs, larvas, and pupas of an ant colony

colony (KOL-uh-nee)—a large group of living things that lives and works together

fungus (FUHN-guhss)—a plantlike living thing that feeds on rotting matter

mandibles (MAN-di-buhls)—the mouthparts of the jaw that are used for biting and gripping

prey (PRAY)—animals that are hunted by other animals for food

thorax (THOR-aks)—the middle part of an insect's body between its head and abdomen

venom (VEN-uhm)—poison produced by snakes, spiders, and some insects

Internet Sites and Addresses

The Ant Colony Cycle
http://mnh.org/entomology/social_insects/ants/
ant_colony_cycle.html

The Ant Farm
http://www.home.apu.edu/~philpi

Myrmecology—The Scientific Study of Ants
http://www.myrmecology.org

Ultimate Guide: Ants
http://www.discovery.com/stories/nature/ants/
ants.html

Rain Forest Action Network
221 Pine Street, Suite 500
San Francisco, CA 94104

Young Entomologists' Society
6907 West Grand River Avenue
Lansing, MI 48906

Index